Anonymous

Men we are proud of

A collection of steel-plate portraits of the chief sctord in our conflict with

Spain

Anonymous

Men we are proud of
A collection of steel-plate portraits of the chief sctord in our conflict with Spain

ISBN/EAN: 9783337231903

Printed in Europe, USA, Canada, Australia, Japan

Cover: Foto ©ninafisch / pixelio.de

More available books at **www.hansebooks.com**

MEN WE ARE PROU

A COLLECTION OF STEEL-PLATE PORTRAITS OF THE CHIEF ACTORS IN OUR CONFLICT WITH SPAIN

With Brief Biographical Sketches

PUBLISHED BY
A. E. FRANCIS AND R. P. STRINE
PHILADELPHIA
1899

Numbered among the immortal lights of history will be the names of America's sons, who played important parts in the war drama recently enacted between Spain and the United States, the climax of which resulted in the downfall of despotism, the freedom of millions, relief of the oppressed, the shouldering of new and mighty responsibilities by our strong young nation and the unfurling of the American flag in distant lands, where it will carry a message of free thought, free speech, free life.

To-day the sun never sets on the starry banner of freedom. Through righteous conquest the United States of America has added to her galaxy of sister states lands that will prove of immense advantage to American commerce. New administrations will soon develop latent energies, and American pluck and enterprise will wrest the richest benefits they can be made to yield from the drowsy embrace of tropical lands.

No nation can, or need be, prouder of her sons. The portraits contained herein depict faithfully and accurately the features of these, our countrymen, who have earned immortal place in the archives of American history. Each subject is the best possible result of the engraver's art, and is of sufficient merit from an artistic view to occupy an honored place.

It is the desire of the publishers to enable the American public to obtain a collection of steel-plate portraits of such evident merit that they will be preserved for their value as art productions as well as for the fame of the personalities they reflect. Nothing has been spared to make these portraits what they should be. They are each the work of an artist, and are entitled to a conspicuous position in every American home.

WILLIAM M'KINLEY

WILLIAM MCKINLEY, the President of the United States, was born in Niles, Ohio, on the 29th of January, 1843. He began his education in the public schools and afterward attended Poland Academy and Allegheny College. Following the completion of his course of studies, and until his enlistment in the army, he taught school. He enlisted as a private in the Twenty-third Ohio Infantry in 1861, and rose through the successive grades until, on March 13, 1865, he was breveted Major of United States Volunteers by President Lincoln for gallantry in battle. In the interval he served on the staffs of Generals R. B. Hayes, G. W. Crook and W. S. Hancock.

He was detailed as Acting Assistant Adjutant General of the First Division of the First Army Corps until he was mustered out on the 26th of July, 1865. He at once took up the study of law in Mahoning County, Ohio; afterward took a course in the Albany, New York, Law School. In 1867 Major McKinley was admitted to the Ohio bar, and in 1869 became the Prosecuting Attorney of Stark County. He served as a member of Congress from 1876 to 1891, and, when Chairman of the Ways and Means Committee in 1890, reported the protective tariff measure popularly known as the "McKinley Bill." He was especially known in Congress as an advocate of a high protective tariff. In 1891 he was elected Governor of Ohio, and re-elected in 1893. Major McKinley was sent as a delegate-at-large to the Republican Convention of 1884, at which he supported Blaine, and in 1888 served in a similar capacity and supported John Sherman for the Presidency. Again, in 1892, he was delegate-at-large, and was made Chairman of the Convention. He refused to allow his own name to be considered, and threw his strength to the renomination of Harrison. At the Republican Convention of 1896 he was nominated for the presidency, and in November of the same year was elected by a popular plurality of 600,000 votes.

His wise administration and conservative policy before and during the Spanish-American War demonstrated clearly his ability to manage his own administration. He made no false moves, and never took a step without careful deliberation. He held Congress in check as long as possible, and when war was declared he acted decisively. President McKinley has proved one of the most popular of Presidents, and has the affection and esteem of the whole American people. No man could have filled his office better or made fewer mistakes. Under his administration the country has enjoyed an era of great prosperity.

GEORGE DEWEY

GEORGE DEWEY, of a prominent Montpelier, Vermont, family, was born there in 1837. At the age of 17 he was appointed to the Naval Academy through his persistency and against his father's poor opinion of sailors. After graduation in 1858 he was assigned to the steam frigate Wabash, of the Mediterranean squadron, and cruised until 1850.

Ensign Dewey was home when Sumter was fired upon. One week later, April 19, 1861, he received his commission as Lieutenant, and was assigned to the steam sloop Mississippi, which was to take part in the fierce fighting of the West Gulf squadron, under the command of Admiral Farragut. The Mississippi was a side-wheeler of seventeen guns; its hardest fight was in trying to run by Port Hudson, with its powerful batteries. She was struck two hundred and fifty times, and in half an hour was as full of holes as a colander. The crew manned the boats on the opposite side from the fort, set the ship on fire and made for the opposite shore.

In July, 1863, Dewey saw more fighting. In 1864 he was attached to the North Atlantic blockading squadron on the steam gunboat Agawam. In 1868 he was assigned to duty at the Naval Academy. In 1870 Admiral Dewey received his first command, the Narragansett. He was on special service until 1875, during which time the Pacific survey was entrusted to him.

A service of two years as Lighthouse Inspector, five years as Secretary of the Lighthouse Board, was succeeded by the command of the Juniata on the Asiatic squadron in 1882. In 1884 he was promoted to Captain in command of the Dolphin. The years 1885 to 1888 found him commanding the Pensacola, the flagship of the European squadron. In 1888 he became Chief of the Bureau of Equipment and Recruiting with rank of Commodore. Admiral Dewey again became a member of the Lighthouse Board in May, 1893, and in 1896 was put at the head of a very important Board, that of Inspection and Survey.

On the first of January, 1898, he was transferred to the command of the Asiatic squadron, flagship Olympia, and five months afterward, May 1, electrified the nation with the greatest naval victory ever known, wiping out the entire Spanish fleet without the loss of a man and only eight men wounded.

At five o'clock on the morning of Sunday, May 1, 1898, the American fleet, under Commodore Dewey, entered the Bay of Manila. On reaching anchorage, Cavite fort opened fire at long range. The Spanish fleet, anchored off Cavite, followed. This action prompted the American ships to draw close in and open a terrible cannonade. At the end of twenty minutes the American fleet again drew into close quarters, the cannonade being rapid and incessant. This terrible onslaught totally destroyed the Spanish fleet. Three of their vessels were burning, one sunk and the others silenced. The land forts were also silenced, making the victory complete. This remarkable battle lasted but three hours and a half, during which time the Spaniards fought bravely against a superior force.

While the above was enacted Dewey, with some of his officers, stood on the forward bridge. His famous remark, "You may fire when ready, Gridley," opened the mouths of the starboard eight-inch gun in the forward turret at 5.41 A. M. at a 5500 yard range.

Congress executed the wish of the American nation by reviving the rank of Admiral and conferring it upon Dewey in recognition of his great victory.

WILLIAM T. SAMPSON

Admiral William T. Sampson was born on what is now known as Morman Hill Farm, in Palmyra, New York, in 1840. He entered the Naval Academy at Annapolis in 1857, graduating shortly before the opening of the Civil War. He served with distinction through the nation's struggle for existence, coming out with the rank of Lieutenant. When the Patapsco, of the blockading fleet before Charleston, was blown up in 1865, young Sampson was her Executive Officer. In 1866, while on the Colorado he received his commision as Lieutenant Commander. He served at the Naval Academy from 1868 to 1871. From 1872 to 1873 he cruised in European waters on the Congress. His first command was the Alert, in 1874, just after attaining the grade of Commander. From 1876 to 1878, he again served at the Naval Academy, and ten years later became Superintendent, in which capacity he served four years.

Since the formation of the New Navy, Admiral Sampson has commanded two of the modern war vessels, the cruiser San Francisco and the battleship Iowa, the latter of which he was the first skipper.

Ordnance matters and torpedo work have received a great amount of special study from him. When the Maine disaster occurred Sampson was appointed President of the Board of Inquiry. His appointment as Commander-in-Chief of the North Atlantic squadron at the beginning of the Spanish-American War, when but a junior officer, was a practical recognition of the quiet, effective seaman, of whom it is said, like Kitchener, "Other Generals have been better loved: none was ever better trusted." He was the right man in the right place, as subsequent events proved. Upon him rested the terrible strain and responsibility which the commanding officer of a blockading squadron must bear.

The whole nation was watching him and waiting to pass judgment. This was the message he cabled the Navy Department, describing, in curt, official language, the great victory on the eve of the nation's liberty day:
"Secretary of Navy—3.15 A. M., Siboney, 3.

"The fleet under my command offers the nation as a Fourth of July present the destruction of Cervera's fleet. No one escaped. It attempted to escape 9.30 A. M., and at 2.00 P. M. the last—the Christobal Colon—had run ashore sixty miles west of Santiago, and had let down her colors. The Infanta Maria Teresa, Oquendo and Viscaya, were forced ashore, burned and blown up, within twenty miles of Santiago. Furor and Pluton were destroyed within four miles of the port. Loss, one killed, two wounded. Enemy's loss, probably several hundred from gun fire, explosions and drowning. About 1300 prisoners, including Admiral Cervera."

Admiral Sampson was not present to direct the fight, having started to inspect the Spanish coast defenses when Cervera came out. His plans and orders, however, were followed to the letter, the battle being fought practically without signals, so thoroughly did the Commanders of the different ships understand the part they had to play.

Since the war he has remained in command of the North Atlantic squadron.

WINFIELD SCOTT SCHLEY

WINFIELD SCOTT SCHLEY was born on October 9, 1839, in Frederick County, Maryland. He comes of an excellent family. At the age of fifteen he entered the Academy at Annapolis, and four years later, after his graduation, he began his seafaring career by making a voyage to Japan as a member of the escort to the Japanese Embassy in 1860. He remained abroad until the breaking out of the Civil War. His gallantry soon won him recognition, and he was placed in command of the first prize ship of the war, the General Parkhill. He served with the Western Gulf squadron in the blockade of Mobile Bay until he was transferred to the gunboat Winona, which patrolled the Mississippi for over a year. At the close of the Civil War Schley was ordered to the Pacific Coast. He was present at the bombardment of Valparaiso and Callao by the Spanish fleet, and was instrumental in suppressing insurrections at Middle Chinca Island and La Union, Honduras. He served abroad in the East India and China squadrons for several years. In 1871 he participated in the attack on the Corean fortifications on the Salee River, leading the assaulting column. In 1884 Admiral Schley headed the Greely relief expedition. On the 15th of April, 1897, he was appointed Chairman of the Lighthouse Board. His reputation for calm, cool-headed judgment and prompt, intrepid action at the right moment was responsible for his assignment as Commander-in-Chief of the famous flying squadron when our trouble with Spain took definite shape. On board the flagship Brooklyn he directed and gave gallant battle on the morning of July 3, when Cervera made his bold and astonishing dash out of Santiago harbor. The responsibility of defeat or success rested with Schley, as second in command, during the absence of his chief, Admiral Sampson. For his gallantry and clearheadedness in this great fight he received his commission as Rear Admiral.

RICHMOND PEARSON HOBSON

RICHMOND PEARSON HOBSON was born on August 17, 1870, in Greensboro, Hale County, Alabama. He was graduated from the Southern University of Greensboro at the head of his class, and appointed to the Naval Academy at Annapolis on competitive examination in May of '85. He was a bright, earnest student who applied himself to such purpose that he finished in 1889 with first honors, notwithstanding his being the youngest man in the class.

His first cruise was on board the flagship Chicago of the Squadron of Evolution commanded by Admiral Walter. It was on this cruise that they visited Brazil and gave recognition to the flag of the Brazilian Republic.

Hobson was soon after ordered abroad to take a special course in the National School of Mines in Paris, followed by a two years course in the Parisian School of Maritime Science. He spent his summer vacation in French shipyards in order to add to his expert knowledge. The French schools awarded him diplomas for distinction in naval construction and design. Before returning to this country Mr. Hobson spent some time in English shipyards.

In 1894 he was assigned to duty in the office of Naval Intelligence and Bureau of Construction and Repairs at Washington. During his term of service in the department he prepared a report of his observations abroad which was discussed with much interest in naval circles. In 1895 Hobson entered the New York Navy Yard as assistant to the Naval Constructor, afterward going with Admiral Bunce on the New York.

It was Hobson who inaugurated a new system of giving sea duty to naval constructors which is of much practical benefit. He also organized and conducted a three years post graduate course at the United States Naval Academy.

On the 17th of April, 1898, Lieutenant Hobson was assigned as Constructor for the fleet stationed at Key West.

During the blockade of the Cuban ports and the manœuvres off Santiago the Naval Board conceived the idea of sinking an obstruction in the channel to prevent the escape of Cervera's fleet, which they believed was penned in. The collier Merrimac was selected as the best available ship for the purpose. Volunteers were called for for the hazardous undertaking, and over four hundred men proffered their services. Hobson begged to be allowed to command the expedition, and accordingly at four o'clock on the morning of June 3, 1898, after he had perfected a well-laid plan, the Merrimac, with a crew of six men and her commander, steamed boldly toward the entrance to the harbor. She was riddled with projectiles, but succeeded in anchoring at the right spot and swung around. When all was ready Hobson set off an internal torpedo by means of an electric attachment. The Merrimac sank instantly, leaving Hobson and his crew to clamber aboard a catamaran which floated clear of the wreck, in which they drifted helplessly to shore. They were made prisoners and conducted to Morro Castle. Cervera sent word to Admiral Sampson, praising the gallantry and bravery of Hobson and his crew and suggesting an exchange, which did not take place until after the war closed.

This one act of bravery has earned for the young Lieutenant a prominent place among America's heroes, and eclipses the blowing up of the Albemarle.

CHARLES DWIGHT SIGSBEE

CHARLES DWIGHT SIGSBEE was born on a farm in Albany County, New York, in the year 1845. At the age of fourteen he received the appointment to the Naval Academy at Annapolis, from which he was graduated in 1863, with the rank of Ensign. On October 1 of the same year he was assigned to the Monongahela, and on that ship and the Brooklyn he served three years in the West Gulf and North Atlantic blockading squadrons. He participated in the Battle of Mobile Bay on the 5th of August, 1864, and in the attacks and final assault on Fort Fisher, losing no opportunity to display great gallantry. Until 1867 he was attached to the Wyoming, doing duty in the Asiatic squadron. On November 10, 1866, Sigsbee received his commission as Master, and on February 21, 1867, became a Lieutenant on the Ashulter. While attached to the Ashulter he received his commission as Lieutenant Commander. In 1869 he was stationed at the Naval Academy, leaving there in 1871 to go on the Worcester, then the flagship of the North Atlantic station. At the close of 1873 Lieutenant Sigsbee assisted in the coast survey, this important work occupying him until 1878, during two years of which he commanded the coast survey steamer Blake. After a four years service as Chief of the Hydrographic Office at Washington he was assigned to the Monadnock; but before the order was put into effect he was transferred to the Maine.

In April, 1897, shortly after going on the Maine, Lieutenant Sigsbee received his commission as Captain.

Lieutenant Sigsbee married during his term of service at the Naval Academy. In 1882, by a joint resolution in Congress, Lieutenant Commander Sigsbee was authorized to accept the decoration of the Red Eagle, tendered by the Emperor of Germany for meritorious services rendered to the German Navy in superintending the construction of a deep-sea machine which he invented.

Captain Sigsbee came into the public eye when his ship, the Maine, was blown up in Havana Harbor on the 15th of February, 1898, and over three hundred of her officers and men perished. The Maine was a second-class battleship, built at the Brooklyn Navy Yard. She was 318 feet long, 57 feet beam, 21.6 mean draught, and 6682 tons displacement. She was equipped with two 10-inch vertical turrets, two military masts, a main battery of four 10-inch and six 6-inch rifles, and secondary battery of seven 6-pounders, eight 1-pound rapid-fire guns, four Gatling guns, and four Whitehead torpedoes. The Maine had a speed of 17.45 knots.

After being without a commission for some time, owing to the disaster of the Maine, Captain Sigsbee was assigned to the command of the converted cruiser St. Paul during the war, and is now in command of the battleship Texas.

CHARLES DWIGHT SIGSBEE

NELSON A. MILES

Nelson A. Miles was born on August 8, 1839, at Westminster, Mass. He began his military career as a Captain of Volunteers in the beginning of the Civil War. He served with distinction in the Army of the Potomac throughout all its campaigns, and through his bravery and gallantry rose to be a Major General of Volunteers. After the close of the Civil War General Miles became a regular army officer in the United States Infantry. He was transferred to the Western frontier, and became one of the greatest of modern Indian fighters, conducting many campaigns, notably against the Apaches under Geronimo and Natchez. His commission as Major General in the regular army dates from April 5, 1890. General Miles enjoys the distinction of being the only soldier in the last fifty years to reach the position of supreme command, which he has occupied since the retirement of General Schofield, without having been graduated from West Point. He is without doubt the best example of the American soldier of the day, and has behind him a record for bravery and ability that justifies his elevation to the prominent office he occupies.

During the railroad strike troubles in Chicago, in 1884, he commanded the United States troops. He represented the United States Army at the seat of the Turco-Grecian War, and also at Queen Victoria's Diamond Jubilee in 1897.

When the war with Spain broke out General Miles, as Commander-in-Chief of the United States Army, assumed command, directing operations from Washington. He afterward shared in the hardships of the Cuban campaign, and on July 21, 1898, sailed from Santiago to invade Puerto Rico, which was numbered among our new possessions before the close of the month. General Miles had prepared for a bloody battle at Arbonita, when the news of the signing of the peace protocol reached him and checked the American artillerymen almost in the act of firing.

General Miles is now under consideration for supreme command in the Phillipines, in the hope of putting a speedy end to the insurgent opposition of Aguinaldo and his followers.

THEODORE ROOSEVELT

One of the best examples of the all-around American is the doughty Colonel of the Rough Riders, Theodore Roosevelt. His career has been one of many phases, and shows him to be honorable, upright, courageous, intelligent, a champion of right, an enemy of corruption, a literary genius and a born leader.

Governor Roosevelt was born in New York on October 27th, 1858. His early education was obtained at Harvard, graduating in 1880. Though but a youngster he plunged into politics and served as a member of the New York Legislature from 1882 to 1884. His next experience was that of an unsuccessful candidate on the Republican ticket for the mayoralty of New York in 1886. He became a member of the National Civil Service Commission in 1889, on which he served until 1895, at which time he was appointed President of the New York Police Board. His efficient term of service there, during which he purged the police machine, was followed by his appointment as Assistant Secretary of the Navy in 1897.

When the Spanish-American War broke out Governor Roosevelt promptly resigned to organize, with Dr. (now General) Leonard E. Wood, the First United States Cavalry Volunteers, which soon became known as "Roosevelt's Rough Riders," owing to its being made up largely of Western Cowboys who knew Roosevelt during his hunting days in the far West for big game. Many members of prominent families and college athletes also became members of the famous organization, which distinguished itself in action during the Cuban campaign. Roosevelt was promoted to a coloneley for gallantry at the battle of La Quasina. After his return to this country he was nominated and elected by a large majority to the Governorship of New York in November, 1898. His bravery, patriotism and fine record in every walk of life made him the logical candidate for Governor, and may yet land him in the White House.

WESLEY MERRITT

Wesley Merritt, Major General, U. S. A., was born June 16, 1836, in New York city. He was graduated from West Point in 1860, and assigned to the dragoons. On May 13, 1861, his rise began by his promotion to a First Lieutenancy. This was followed by a Captaincy in April, 1862, a promotion for bravery to Brevet Major General, on March 13, 1865, and the rank of Lieutenant Colonel on July 26, 1866. Since the Civil War he has been regularly promoted through the successive steps to the rank of Major General. During the War of the Rebellion he was commissioned a Major General of the volunteer service.

General Merritt served in the Army of the Potomac, and was promoted a number of times for gallantry. He participated in the Gettysburg fight, at Yellow Tavern, Hawe's Shop, Five Forks, etc.; accompanied General Sheridan on his cavalry raid toward Charleston, and was engaged in the Battle of Trevilian Station. In the Shenandoah campaign Merritt commanded the cavalry division from August, 1864, to March, 1865. He figured in the battles of Winchester and Fisher's Hill; he also commanded a corps of cavalry in the Appomatox campaign. General Merritt was one of the three commanders from the Union Army elected to confer with the Confederate commanders for the surrender of the Army of Northern Virginia. After the war he served in various departments, participated in several Indian campaigns, was Superintendent of the United States Military Academy from 1882 to 1887. Following that he was appointed to the command of the Department of the Atlantic, and served in that capacity until the breaking out of the Spanish-American War, when he was assigned, in May, 1898, to the command of the United States forces in the Phillipine Islands, arriving there on July 25th, followed by a force of 50,000 soldiers.

On August 13, a day after the peace protocol had been signed in Paris, the American soldiers assaulted the city at Malate, while Admiral Dewey opened up a fierce bombardment of the capital of Luzon. The foe was quickly driven into the inner walls, from which soon floated the white flag of surrender. After establishing a form of military government in Manila, General Merritt went to Paris to inform the Peace Commission of the status in the Phillipines. Upon his return to this country he again took command of the Department of the Atlantic.

WESLEY MERRITT

ROBLEY DUNGLISON EVANS

Robley D. Evans, Captain, United States Navy, better known as "Fighting Bob" Evans, was born in Floyd County, Va. His early education was obtained in the Washington public schools, when, in September, 1860, he was appointed to the United States Naval Academy from Utah Territory. He was graduated from there in 1863, receiving his commision as Ensign in October of the same year. This was followed by his promotion to a lieutenancy in July, 1866; Lieutenant Commander, March, 1868; Commander, July, 1878, and Captain, June 27, 1893.

During the Civil War Captain Evans participated in both attacks on Fort Fisher, in January, 1865, and in the land attack received four severe rifle wounds.

When in command of the Yorktown at Valpariaso, Chili, during the period of the strained relations between that country and the United States, in 1891, his actions in connection with the various incidents earned him the popular sobriquet of "Fghting Bob." He was also in the public eye as the bosom friend of former President Cleveland. During our war with Spain Captain Evans commanded the battleship Iowa in Admiral Sampson's fleet off Santiago, and took an active part in the battle with Cervera's fleet on July 3, 1898. He is now in command of the Iowa, one of the ships of the North Atlantic squadron.

www.ingramcontent.com/pod-product-compliance
Lightning Source LLC
Chambersburg PA
CBHW021456090426
42739CB00009B/1751

* 9 7 8 3 3 3 7 2 3 1 9 0 3 *